SELF-ESTEEM FOR WOMEN

A Psychologist's Guide to Overcome Self-Doubt, Stress & Anxiety - How to Build Confidence & Happiness Instead

KATHERINE CHAMBERS

TABLE OF CONTENTS

INTRODUCTION

"If I could give you one gift, I would give you the ability to
see yourself as I see you, so you could see how truly
special you are"

(Anonymous)

Lets face it, very few of us are blessed with high levels of natural self-esteem. Humans are flawed by our very nature, but that's OK. That's what makes life interesting. To continually fight to overcome these limitations and come out the other side all the better for it. I grant you that for most, this is easier said than done. The negative conditioning we absorb through the years, especially with regards to ourselves, can really hinder our thinking. It can stifle our progress, and often cause us much undue mental anguish along the way.

But it wasn't always like this. As toddlers we had none of these worries. We were ruthless in getting what we wanted, without the slightest inkling that we didn't deserve what we were screaming for. We crawled all day long trying to reach our feet. There was never a thought of "I'm not good enough for this walking stuff, I'll just give up". We continued on until we'd achieved it, without a seconds hesitation.

However, the conditioning soon starts to change. From the ages of 2-8 we begin to pick up all sorts of programming about the world. We start to evaluate our surroundings, and more importantly, how we fit into them. We begin to ascribe meaning to events, which can have huge implications over time. This continues into our teenage years and young adult life. Its then simply a game of gauging our place in the social pecking order. This can be especially true for women, as the societal pressures are so heavy.

I have long been obsessed with uncovering the principles which most effectively lead to a harmonious life. My own has been a testing ground for these tenets. Self-reflection, self-reliance, persistence in overcoming adversity and so on. All of these attributes contribute to a well rounded individual. But they essentially all serve to feed into one place, the characteristic which has the biggest impact on your life I.e. increased levels of overall confidence and self-worth. These traits underpin every aspect of your personality, and subsequent behaviors. If anything, this book is designed to get you back to the natural and pure success seeking mindset you had as a toddler.

If you have read any of my other work then you know who I am by now, so I'll save you the background credibility check here. I'd rather we dive straight into correcting low self-esteem if that's OK with you. Again, there simply isn't a more beneficial psychological topic to discuss in my opinion, especially when it comes to women. The following chapters will give you some in-depth insight into the principles which lead to self-doubt, anxiety and even depression. But more importantly, advice on how to overcome these circumstances. So lets waste no further time and dive in.

PART 1: A BASIC UNDERSTANDING OF SELF-ESTEEM

CHAPTER 1: SELF-ESTEEM VS SELF-CONFIDENCE

"Confidence comes from not always being right, but from not fearing to be wrong"

(Peter Mcintyre)

Self-esteem is often described as self-judgment. It refers to the overall notion of personal value or self-worth. It's comprised of various ideas regarding oneself, such as the assessment of appearance, emotions, behaviors and principles. Essentially, self-esteem is simply as measure of how much you appreciate yourself, and how well you can operate throughout the day, despite the external and internal hardships you will face.

High overall self-esteem is critical to achieving a harmonious life. Its the driver which underpins all positive behavior patterns. You can't achieve anything without first believing that you deserve to have it, and this is exclusively linked to your own self-worth. Its a little different compared to say pure confidence for instance. There's a slight but significant difference between the two.

Some would argue that we are merely debating semantics here, but I determine confidence as more of a state trait. It's more closely linked with competence in a given area or task. We all feel confident in some settings, but not in others. Confidence is typically determined by proficiency which comes with practice and repetition. Do you feel confident when you first get behind the wheel of a car? Do you feel comfortable giving a speech in front of 50 colleagues for the first time? Of course not. But drive everyday for 10 years or give a 100 speeches and its a different story.

Self-esteem however runs deeper than this. It goes beyond situational states of competence. It transcends any situation you may find yourself in. It pertains to the internal feelings and emotional components of a persons personality, which I described previously. In this sense, increasing your overall self-worth is a very worthwhile thing to do, as it positively effects every area of your life. Its a tide which raises all boats so to speak.

I would argue that there really is no downside to ever increasing levels of self-esteem. You simply love yourself and the others around you just that much more each day. Some will talk about achieving a level of balance, but I would suggest they are again referring to self-confidence, or more accurately, grandiose levels of self-importance.

There is definitely a downside to taking yourself too seriously, but also not seriously enough. Operating at either end of this extreme confidence spectrum can be detrimental in opposing ways. This is why I want to touch upon this briefly before moving onto the specific tenets of developing true self-worth. In an ideal situation, those with high levels of self-esteem would also have healthy levels of self-confidence. But that's not always the case.

The Importance of Balance When it Comes to Confidence

People with extremely low levels of self-confidence often deal with frequent feelings of defeat and depression. They tend to get pulled into situations wherein they make bad choices, plain and simple. They settle for unhealthy relationships and fail to be the best versions of themselves. Something always holds them back from succeeding, due mainly to the lack of necessary self-beliefs which trigger self-sabotaging behavior.

On the other hand, people with an overblown sense of self-confidence can prove to be very obnoxious and oftentimes intolerable. They tend to think of themselves as better than everyone else, which prevents them from cultivating healthy personal and professional relationships alike. They refuse to admit when they are wrong and habitually blame everyone but themselves for their own shortcomings.

Again, there's a fine line here. I often hear people say things like "I'm often wrong, but never in doubt". On one hand this serves as a great success mindset to have. It allows a person to push forward with little to no distractions in their mind. It affords a focus critical to getting big goals achieved. However, it can be highly annoying to the surrounding people when a person gets too entrenched in a position without ever taking a self-critical view on things.

These people are extremely competitive and always striving to get ahead of the pack. They view material and monetary success as their main source of happiness, but their attitude simply makes true happiness elusive. Unsurprisingly, all of the aforementioned traits make it very difficult to establish affectionate and healthy relationships with those around them. They view everyone as an opponent to be overthrown in the continual competition of life.

Those who exhibit low self-esteem on the other hand, do the exact opposite. They fail to see their worth, they cannot acknowledge their capabilities, and these insecurities always loom in every situation they find themselves in. They are constantly fearful of failing which holds them back. They take a different route, but ultimately end up in the same place of unhappiness.

A healthy self-confidence can be found somewhere in the middle of these extremes. Its having the realistic confidence in one's own skills and abilities. Its in reaching an "unconscious competence" level of proficiency of a task. You know exactly what you can do, as well as the things that you cannot in any particular moment. However, you are not inhibited by this. You are aware of your strengths and weaknesses, and you know how to maximize them in order to get closer to your ultimate goals.

Healthy levels of self-confidence ensures a person feels secure enough to withstand unfavorable events and failures. Its worth noting, that maintaining this kind of state takes a lifetime of work and dedication to tasks. There will be moments when insecurities can arise, especially in competitive contexts. The mind is never static, so the key to self-confidence therein lies in having the constant motivation to learn how life's adversities can be overcome. This takes a continual effort to push the boundaries of ones own comfort zone.

How Self-Esteem Develops

So having explored the notion of overall self-confidence, its now time to switch gears. Its time to assess what it means to have true self-esteem or self-worth (I'll use these terms interchangeably as they are generally describing the same thing).

Self-esteem is an essential element for maintaining your overall well-being. It will play a significant role in our attempts to form healthy and positive relationships as we go through life. In fact, our view of our adult self is highly influenced by how we lived as children. It goes back to infancy and gradually develops as time passes by. A healthy self-esteem can be established early on in a child's life simply by making him or her feel safe, accepted, and genuinely loved. Its long been known that virtually all of our personality traits and feelings of self-worth are developed during this time.

From the age of 2 years up until around 6-7, children are like sponges, they absorb everything. EEG pattern studies indicate that they spend much of this time in high frequency theta brain wave states. This explains why they can learn at rapid rates, even picking up multiple languages simultaneously with relative ease.

A friend of mine visited Amsterdam a few years back and was surprised to find she could loosely understand the locals when they are talking to one another. On returning to the States she told the story to her parents, who reminded her that she spent most of her days as a toddler with a nanny from Holland. It turned out this lady used to speak Dutch to my friend when she looked after her. But English when her parents got home from work. The remnants of the language had remained in her subconscious mind all of this time.

More critically though, we also attribute meaning to things and situations during those formative years which forms our base paradigms for viewing the world. How are parents and siblings react to us has a monumental impact on our behavior into adolescence and then adult life. Things which often need to be re-visited in order to rectify deeply held notions of self-worth, or lack there of. For the majority of people I meet, low levels of self-esteem can almost always be tracked back to some form of neglect as a child. Or some form of miss appropriation of meaning from menial events when growing up.

In fact, everything in childhood will affect a persons eventual level of elf-esteem. Each time a child tries to do and learn new things is an opportunity for them to develop higher degrees of self-worth, such as:

- Learning new concepts in school

- Acquiring new skills (art, music, sports, cooking, etc.)

- Making new friends

- Getting feedback on behavior, good and bad

Children who know how to feel good about themselves will grow into adults who are confident enough to try out new things. They will know how to deal with mistakes, and failure will not prevent them from getting up and trying again. I write about this re-contextualization more thoroughly within "Jealousy: A Psychologists Guide". But its certainly safe to say that this stems from childhood by and large.

Did your parents ever warn you of the dangers in life? Did they ever stress the importance of looking both ways before crossing the street? They likely did, and they are well within their rights to do so. Protecting a child is paramount to any parent, but what they are subconsciously communicating is "the world is a scary place, watch out for dangers at every turn". Its no wonder we grow up not ever wanting to take the slightest of risks.

If you read some of the autobiographies of the worlds most successful entrepreneurs, they all have one thing in common. Their parents did the opposite of the above. Richard Branson grew up on a farm in the British countryside wherein his mother would instruct him to go out and find adventure each day. To go out and explore the world. Its no coincidence that his net worth is now north of $5 billion.

Dr Benjamnin Spock was one of the first American pediatricians to study the psychoanalysis of children. He wrote a book in 1946 titled "The Common Sense Book of Baby & Childcare" which fast became a best seller. Among other great advice contained within the book, the central theme was predominantly based around how to communicate with children. Specifically how to negotiate requests and never to say "No" to them. But rather explore the avenues of their questions and the implications they might have. To get them to think more critically, but importantly, so they don't grow up with negative connotations to being turned down for what they want.

Studies show that parents who implemented these techniques went on to raise some of the most well-rounded and successful children measured for every metric of success. By contrast, children who develop low self-esteem during these formative years, will often feel unsure of themselves. They may always harbour a feeling of inadequacy and be more vulnerable to mistreatment later in life. They are more prone to bullying and poor treatment from others in high school and later on within the workplace.. They don't handle mistakes and set-back nearly as well as they might.

That being said, none of this is an excuse for continual bad behavior and poor performance. Yes much of our mental patterns, including those feelings of self-worth are anchored to our early years. But they are NOT set in stone. We can certainly do something about them with a little effort and the correct guidance. While negative thoughts and self-talk is not something that can't be unlearned overnight, we can work on reversing this trend. The second part to this book is designed to help you do just that.

CHAPTER 2: WHY DO WOMEN SUFFER POOR SELF IMAGE?

"Self-esteem is the most fragile attribute in human nature. It can be damaged by very minor incidents, and its reconstruction is often difficult to engineer"

(Dr. James Dobson)

Self-esteem is fundamental to identity, and a critical ingredient in anyone's ability to feel genuine happiness. It helps us feel validated from within, but sometimes, despite having a strong resolve, this self-worth can be toppled by external forces. Women are especially susceptible to this as the media and society at large control what is "acceptable", particularly in terms of appearance, behavior, and societal roles.

Society and Negative Self-Image

There's no getting away from it, popular consensus highly regards "thinness" as a factor of beauty in this day and age. Whilst this perception may be changing somewhat in recent years, I would still argue this notion holds true in the minds of most women. Its often portrayed to go hand-in-hand with success, wealth, and social status. We see images of slender women in almost every form of media - magazines, on television, billboards, movies and so on. Due to this constant bombardment, many women are driven to believe that achieving this level of appearance is the answer to getting everything they wish from life.

The subconscious mind reverts to the habit of comparing yourself to others in this regard. Friends, family and significant others also play their part. These people may frequently and explicitly tell you less than favorable things about the way you look. It can be difficult to ignore these individuals entirely. Your close and constant proximity to them, in addition to valuing their opinions by default, makes it easy to spiral down into negative thinking if you are not careful.

Another culprit worth mentioning is the highly influential and profitable weight loss industry. Whilst some of these companies do have our best interests at heart, especially the more nutritionally based and health centric businesses. Others simply exist to sell us false dreams of a better life by counting calories, or worse, crash dieting. They thrive on our insecurities which ultimately results in us purchasing their products and trying their fade diets in order to achieve our dreams for the small fee of $49!

They are banking on the belief that we are not enough, and they are on hand to help, that their weight loss products and programs can make us feel happy and complete once more. Whilst its a good idea to exercise regularly and eat clean foods to maintain a healthy weight, it should primarily be done for the sake of better health, and not to seek validation from others.

Body Image Awareness

Body image is all about how we see our physical selves. A distorted body image is an unrealistic perception of one's own body. The official term is body dysmorphia, and we all have it to some degree. For most women, its a simple an easy thing to manage with a little rationality and common sense. Growing comfortable in your own skin also very much comes with maturity.

Much like overall self-esteem in general, negative body image can stem from childhood experiences, as well as an unhealthy comparison with the rest of society later in life. Of course friends and family also play a role here. Even though you may fall within the normal weight range, a distorted body image can result from statements like, "if you just lose those last 5 lbs, you'd look really great". These seemingly well intentioned and subtle suggestions can have a big impact over time, if you do not learn to manage your thoughts properly.

Not ever feeling attractive enough is an exhausting emotion to harbor. The question therefore may be. "Is there a way to stop being too critical of your physical appearance? Will there be a time when you won't obsess about the tiniest of flaws?" Again, this somewhat comes with age, but if you wish to combat this in a more proactive manner, the following are the warning signs of negative or distorted body image to watch out for:

- Being overly observant of your features when looking in mirrors

- Obsessively comparing yourself to others

- Being constantly envious of role model's and celebrities

Just like problems with low self-esteem, a negative body image isn't something to be solved by sweeping it under the rug. In order for proper recovery to take place, its important to recognize the problem to begin with. To acknowledge the negative feelings that you are currently dealing with. To discover how to make your body feel comfortable, whilst eradicating the irrational thoughts of not being enough.

Movement and dance therapy are great alternative methods to improve one's body image. They can be used as a tool to help build trust and appreciate your body through creative expression and experimentation. It will feel strange and uncomfortable at first, but I have seen many women flower once just a small degree of competence is achieved. Its a liberating practice with so many confidence building and health related benefits.

Poor Self-Image and Relationships

As I have already pointed out, today's beauty standards can be extremely high and demanding for the average person to achieve. We are all different and should be encouraged to embrace these differences. Often times we can't help but aspire to these ideals, to have that perfect physique or face, too resemble that actress or TV presenter.

We intuitively know that it's really what's on the inside that matters. Our physical bodies shouldn't have to be a determining factor of our worth, nor should it overbearingly affect the way we feel about ourselves. However, this is a difficult concept to grasp for most, especially those who already have a poor self-image. More often than not, they are already dealing with feelings of self-hate and worthlessness, and they may well be on their way to triggering depression or developing an eating disorder in extreme cases.

In this sense, a negative self-image is going to have a huge impact on relationships, no matter what kind. It will affect how we feel and how we interact with others on every level. This almost always puts undue pressure on couples. In a romantic relationship, the partner of someone who has a negative self-image will usually offer words of encouragement to counter the negativity, hoping to solve the problem. Although, even the most well-intentioned words and honest compliments will fall on deaf ears to those with a poor self-image. This will spark additional tensions and inevitably cause the relationship suffer.

It can also affect a couple's intimacy. Someone who doesn't feel satisfied about the way they look, will typically struggle with intimacy. Feelings of unattractiveness and low self-confidence will cause them to second-guess their partner's feelings and attraction towards them. They may feel uncomfortable being touched or being naked in front of them.

If you feel that you are dealing with poor self-image, and you notice that it's already affecting your relationships and life in general, you should consider having a self-image makeover. Here are some of the things you can do to achieve this, albeit slowly:

1. Choose to see your accomplishments

Dwelling on your outer appearance all the time isn't going to do you any good. You don't look like anybody else, and if you keep on comparing yourself to those around you, there will always be moments when you are going to fall short. Instead of nitpicking all your physical flaws, channel your energy into reminding yourself of what you're good at.

2. Say no to negative self-talk

Women can be extremely critical of themselves; somehow, it's easy for us to see our flaws when we look in the mirror. Whilst we already know that no one is perfect and that there will always be details we wish we could change about ourselves, the ability to accept oneself wholly is what truly sets the happy people apart from those who have a negative self-image.

This isn't going to be an overnight change of course. The transition from negative to positive thinking can take some time, so you have to be patient with yourself. Keep those negative thoughts at bay, and do a little more each day to build that snowball of positive self-image bit-by-bit.

3. Take baby steps

If you are really dissatisfied with your physical appearance to the point that even shifting your thoughts isn't working, your list of viable solutions for achieving happiness will become shorter. You can try harder and be more patient when fully accepting yourself, or you can do something to change what you dislike about your body by focusing on one small change at a time.

Instead of signing up for the gym, dance class and new diet plan all in one go. Knock each off one month at a time. Start with just 30 minutes of exercise per day for the first month, walking, cycling or swimming etc. Then add in that Pilates class once a week the following month. Once you have these activities fully rocking, start improving your diet with cleaner carbohydrates and reduced sugar meals. Taking on these tasks one at a time makes them exponentially easier to achieve, and more critically more sustainable in the long term.

4. Open yourself up to others

This will be the most difficult for some, but if you want to stop viewing yourself in such a negative light, you need to start letting the people around you know how you truly feel. This is required all the more if you are in a committed relationship. Your significant other shouldn't be kept in the dark about the anxieties you feel regarding your self-image. You need to open up to them, and in doing so, they'll better understand what you're going through, as well as the reasons for your actions and behaviors. The more they know, the more they'll be able to figure out a way to help you get through your troubles.

Sometimes, even the support of loved ones may fall short in talking you out of your negative self-image. In such instances, it might be best to talk to a counselor about your feelings. A professional's opinions can help you gain a better perspective of your situation and they can teach you how to manage your negative thoughts. They will be able to help you understand what triggers your poor self-image, and lead you to solutions that can greatly improve how you see yourself.

These seemingly small steps can be the change you need in order to make a big difference in getting your happiness back on track. The key is to integrate small changes into your life little by little in ways that are not overwhelming, but will definitely help you gain a healthier disposition each day. Regaining a more healthy self-image is a marathon not a sprint. Making just a 1% improvement each week will compound into a huge improvement in no time at all.

CHAPTER 3: WARNING SIGNS YOU MAY BE SUFFERING FROM AN INFERIORITY COMPLEX

"Having a low opinion of yourself is not modesty. It's self destruction"

(Bobby Sommer)

Much like poor self-image, feelings of general inferiority are very common, but few are open to discussing it. Some are able to push through and eventually gain self-confidence, although not without struggle. Oftentimes these are just momentary feelings which can be overcome before long. However, people who are unable to get past these episodes tend to develop a serious inferiority complex. This condition typically starts once again during childhood, and will translate into adult life if not treated early enough.

These individuals tend to be extremely sensitive people who constantly put themselves down. While some had the chance to accept, acknowledge, and conquer their limitations as they matured, many get stuck, not knowing how to solve them. They may have been raised in authoritarian households where they were always reminded of their flaws. These can include anything from physical appearance, academic ability, sporting prowess and so on.

As a result of the constant reminders of their perceived inadequacies, they typically begin to show symptoms of an inferiority complex. Usually, this manifests in the form of defense mechanisms expressed each time they feel inferior.

Low Self-Esteem and Quality of Life

Inferiority complexes and low self-esteem go hand-in-hand. Both involve feelings of worthlessness and not being able to make the grade. Having to deal with either or both can lead to a multitude of problems, some of which we may not even be conscious of. These feelings are already difficult enough to deal with, but they can engulf us and dictate our every action if we are not careful. Even positively perceived situations can be turned into negatives due to low self-esteem. For many, its a cycle.

Connecting with others on a deeper level may once again become an issue. Feelings of inferiority are going to creep up and make you feel ashamed of yourself. Thus, it can be difficult to open up to others out of fear they will view your vulnerability. You tend to distance yourself from everyone as you can't risk having them see the parts you may be shameful of.

More often than not, you will also worry that others are judging you harshly. It causes a person to become stressed and anxious each time they interact with others. They are constantly scared of saying something wrong, having nothing to say, or simply being uninteresting to people. They will then be inclined to believe they aren't good enough as they can't meet the social expectations they've set for themselves.

Feelings of Inadequacy

Have you ever heard or said any of the following things?

- I'm not good enough for this

- I don't think I deserve it

- Everyone is just better at this than I am

A person who feels inadequate would usually say something along those lines. Later on we will discuss how to reverse these negative statements and self-talk with super positive affirmations. Feelings of inadequacy often arise from the belief that others are inherently better than you, or that you are simply incompetent by nature. People tend to underestimate themselves and sell themselves short as they don't have the required confidence to feel they bring adequate value to the table. Sound familiar?

Oftentimes, people need not hear any verbal judgment to feel this way. All they need to do is misinterpret certain events or actions, and those things can trigger a downward spiral of feeling inadequate. For example, they may presume people are whispering behind their backs or looking at them strangely when the truth is, they are simply busy minding their own business. Even if they are the subject of those conversations or gazes, it's never as negative as the affected individuals make it seem.

Before you can address your issues of inadequacy, you need to get to the root of those feelings first. Do you believe your personality is boring? Or perhaps you feel unattractive and have nothing to offer the opposite sex? Each person's reasons for feeling inadequate will be different. When you get to exploring your own, you have a much higher chance of finding the most appropriate method to drive those emotions away.

It takes a certain degree of courage to come face-to-face with such undesirable feelings. Sometimes you will be required to dig deep into your subconscious to learn where all your insecurities are coming from. To go back to those childhood memories to see where you picked up this psychological baggage. You may have to make your mind go to places it doesn't want to visit in order to get to the root of the problem.

If you are harboring feelings of inferiority and inadequacy all the time, then it might be wise to start becoming more proactive about seeking help. Its in your best interests to go back and unpack these instances, when you felt you lacked in areas which mattered to you. Although it can be a truly uncomfortable experience, the self-understanding you will gain will provide the wisdom required in order to move forward.

Warning Signs of an Inferiority Complex

Many people, particularly women, are not so sure of themselves due to the many outdated thoughts on "acceptability" which still prevail in our society today. Often times its our very traditions which keep people from breaking free from such obsolete stereotypes. In order for anyone to walk towards healthy change, it will be of great help to identify these warning signs of an inferiority complex first and foremost. The main symptoms are as follows:

1. Increased sensitivity to other people's views

Individuals who are dealing with inferiority complexes are highly sensitive to both criticisms and compliments. They are quick to become defensive when they are criticized, and they tend to question the sincerity of a person's words when complimented. Even light humor can make them uncomfortable. Also, they tend to take things too personally, including insignificant passing comments.

2. Social withdrawal

They may also be socially withdrawn as they view everyone as being better than they are, they never feel truly worthy when in large groups. They'd rather be alone and keep their thoughts to themselves. This one is more difficult to overcome for the naturally introverted.

3. Blaming everything and everyone but themselves

When they mess-up, they blame everything on external factors like bad luck, bad company, the environment, or even the universe. They fail to take responsibility and will never admit or accept that the failure may largely be due to their own doing. Their failures and miseries are caused by all the things and people around them, but never themselves.

4. Excessive attention seeking

There is also a high probability to behave in excessively attention-seeking ways. They will annoyingly frame conversations in a manner which makes others compliment them, yet they quickly refute these kind words in order to receive additional validation. Because they crave recognition so much, they will do anything to get people to notice them, even if it's in a negative light. They may act aggressively, appear depressed, or pretend to be unwell for the sake of such coveted attention.

Awareness of a problem's warning signs is one of the first steps to solving it. The sooner that we're able to accept that we're dealing with something which is causing trouble for us, the sooner we'll be able to make the necessary changes to make things right.

In reality, overall low self-esteem, poor self-image, negative body issues and legitimate inferiority complexes, are inextricably linked. Having one almost always means having at least an element of another. The good news is that they are all fixed in exactly the same way. By implementing some cognitive tricks to begin viewing yourself in a much more positive light. We'll get to what these are soon don't worry...

CHAPTER 4: UNDERSTANDING ANXIETY & DEPRESSION

"Nothing can bring you peace but yourself"

(Ralph Waldo Emmerson)

So having explored some of the factors which make us prone to self-esteem issues, as well as how this can play out with regards to tendencies in our behavior. Its wise to take a look at the final area where this can be a problem. The place where low levels of self-worth and inferiority complexes can arise. Unfortunately this can all too commonly end up in anxiety and depression.

Clinical psychologists spend much of their time treating these two instances in patients, as they are so prevalent in today's world. They effect each of us to varying degrees at some stage in life. The likelihood is just far greater if you are predisposed to low self-esteem. The aim of this book is to hopefully help you avoid the worst of these conditions by dealing with your personality traits in a positive manner. But lets first take a look at these more serious mental conditions to begin with.

Anxiety in a Nutshell

Anxiety is defined as the body's normal reaction to perceived stressful events. It's the feeling of distress and unease a person typically experiences prior to a big event which is on the horizon. For example, that jittery sensation a person feels before performing in front of a crowd, or the unrest someone automatically feels before taking an important exam. This is actually healthy anxiety. It aids a person in staying focused and alert, providing a positive overall effect on performance.

When Anxiety Becomes a Problem

Not everyone is fortunate enough to experience just this normal form of anxiety, some will suffer from Anxiety Disorder. A legitimate condition which requires careful consideration by a health care professional. It's a type of mental disturbance wherein a person suffers from irrational anxiety, which has gone overboard. Its usually expressed as an excessive and inappropriate response to a current situation, or anticipated future event.

People with anxiety disorder experience episodes which suddenly creep into their thinking. It consumes them, often in normal, everyday situations. Anxiety disorders can also recur often, and sufferers feel as if they have completely lost all control when these anxious impulses do arise. There are in fact a number of ways in which these moments can come to light. The following are conditions which can be classified as anxiety disorders:

1. **Panic Attacks**

2. **Social Anxiety Disorder**

3. **Separation Anxiety**

4. **Phobias**

5. **Generalized Anxiety Disorder**

The specific symptoms a person may exhibit will vary depending on their particular disturbance. But there are common symptoms which most sufferers share. They include the following:

- Sudden and uncontrollable feelings of panic and worry

- Sweaty and cold hands and feet

- Restlessness

- Muscle tension

- Heart palpitations

- Inability to concentrate

- Dry mouth

- Shortness of breath

- Nausea

- Dizziness

- Tingling and numbness of the hands and feet

Causes of Anxiety Disorders

Anxiety disorders may stem from various causes, depending on the person and their individual circumstances. The causes could be a mixture of several physical and chemical factors happening within the person's body. Contrary to popular belief, anxiety disorders are not predominantly caused by improper upbringing or character weakness. Rather, the following factors are more influential in causing them:

- Dysfunction within the regions of the brain related to fear and stress regulation

- Changes in the brains memory regulating centers

- Chemical imbalances

- Genetic or hereditary factors

- Long-standing stress

- Substance and/or alcohol abuse

- Medication side-effects

- Other related mental health issues that may cause a flare-up of anxiety

Treating Anxiety

People with anxiety disorders must have their negative thoughts slowly altered and replaced with positive ones. This enables them to perceive and associate more positive emotions with regards to the things they're anxious of. By changing the way a person thinks about their fears and anxieties, they can simultaneously change the way they feel and behave towards the situation. This is known as "Cognitive Restructuring" or "Thought Challenging". Here, the therapist identifies a client's negative thoughts and challenges them through three steps:

1. Identifying the person's negative thoughts.

2. Challenging them through evaluation, then finding evidence to disprove the negative thoughts.

3. Introducing more rational and realistic thoughts to replace the negative ones.

Depression Explained

First of all, it's important to state that its normal to feel sad and down at times. Sadness is a normal human emotion which people feel as a result of momentary life struggles and/or the loss of something or someone. It's an inescapable facet of life.

But clinical depression is different. This prevalent mental disturbance goes far beyond the typical down days everyone experiences from time to time. Clinical depression, also known as major depressive disorder, is defined as an overwhelming feeling of intense sadness that can last for weeks or even months at a time, and acutely hinders a person's daily activities in every sense.

Diagnosing Clinical Depression

The key hallmarks of true depression are continuing depressed moods and a notable diminishing of any interest in activities which a person previously enjoyed doing. Either of these symptoms must be present in a person on a daily basis, or almost daily for two weeks in order for it to be confirmed as clinical depression.

In addition to this, depression can also be diagnosed using the guidelines in the DSM-5 Manual. If a person experiences at least five of the following eight symptoms, for a minimum of two weeks, then they can be considered clinically depressed:

1. Depressed mood throughout the entire day, but most markedly during mornings.

2. A huge loss of interest in previously enjoyed activities.

3. Repetitive suicidal thoughts.

4. Intense feelings of guilt and worthlessness.

5. Unrelenting restlessness.

6. Inability to concentrate and make decisions.

7. Sudden surge of weight loss or weight gain.

8. Frequent insomnia occurring daily or almost daily.

A person exhibiting these symptoms will often appear physically distressed and/or impaired. Note that these symptoms must stand on their own and must not be caused by a side effect of any other medication, in order to truly pass as clinical depression. They must also not be a direct result of a preexisting medical condition.

It's also important to note, that nobody can be completely inoculated from feeling this way. It can happen to anyone, regardless of their socio-economic status or standing in life. Even if a person lives in total comfort and has all of the monetary and material wealth in the world, they are still not immune from developing depression.

True clinical depression is not something to be taken lightly. Anyone who considers themself at risk from experiencing this condition, should consult a health care professional as soon as possible. Low overall self-esteem is not the same thing as depression, but can lead us down that road if we are not careful. Therefore, the remainder of this book is dedicated to helping you combat these negative emotions of low self-worth within yourself. To prevent yourself from ever getting close to feeling this way to begin with.

PART 2: SELF-ESTEEM - TECHNIQUES & PRACTICAL STRATEGIES TO BOOST YOUR LEVELS

CHAPTER 5: DEVELOPING BETTER THINKING PATTERNS

"Take care how you speak to yourself, because you are listening"

(Anonymous)

It's extremely important to be vigilant with regards to your thoughts and feelings when initially attempting to raise your overall levels of self-esteem. To become an emotionally stable individual, you have to be aware of what is going on inside of you at all times. There is no right or wrong assumptions to be made to begin with. Like everyone else, your emotions will be a mixture of irrational reactions by and large.

Humans typically elicit emotional responses easily and swiftly in almost every situation, and suppressing them is a tough task. But that's OK. This is just the start. It's about identification and recognition of these feelings to begin with. Especially when they are negative in nature regarding your personality or physical traits, as they can so easily lead to negative spirals of thinking.

This is the brains default position. Humans are very much hardwired to focus on the negative. We zero in on the potential dangers we face, as it was so important to do so from an evolutionary standpoint. Our survival was dependant on directing urgent attention towards negative outcomes. If you attributed the rustling in the bushes to the movements of a saber-toothed tiger, then you had time to react. If you dismissed it as the wind, and it wasn't, then you were removed from the gene pool.

It's officially known as the "Negativity Bias" to psychologists. It explains how we inherently focus on the unpleasant thoughts and emotions such as harmful and traumatic events. This is true even when we are presented with an equal amount of neutral or positive situations. Negative factors have a much greater and disproportionate effect on a persons psychological state. It takes 5-7 positive thoughts, just to balance out a single negative emotion!

In this sense, we have a tendency to profess over the downsides we view within ourselves. Over thinking these traits is certainly not a wise thing to do. If you are not careful you can get trapped in your own mind. This is especially relevant when contemplating undesirable attributes.

In fact, a person with genuinely high levels of self-esteem, will learn to quiet the mind for the majority of the day. They will use their cognitive ability wisely, and simply to plan the necessary tasks they have to complete. To organize their routines before getting back to relative calm and stillness of thought. They largely use the brain for what it is, a tool at their disposal.

The brain is undoubtedly a complex organ. Its required to perform an incredible number of calculations every second, even during mundane tasks like guiding the body for movement in simple motor skills, all the way up to making crucial and complex decisions in real time. The brain undertakes millions of these interconnected decisions every single day, thereby making it one of the most powerful pieces of biological machinery we have.

So it should be used wisely and with care, especially when it comes to developing thought patterns and habits which ultimately dictate our daily behaviors and thinking patterns. It does this in an attempt to optimize a person's day-to-day movements and thought processes, but these short cuts aren't always beneficial.

The formation of these pathways is known as neuroplasticity. Neurology has intrigued scientists & psychologists greatly over the past two centuries. From the Classical Conditioning described by Pavlov and John Watson, to the Operant Conditioning of B. F Skinner. Each presented theories which described how the human brain works and learns.

Its no secret that a person's daily habits and thinking routines will ultimately dictate how they view themselves. However habits are impartial, they will either help a person attain their desired results, or they will ensure they continue getting the average/poor results they have always gotten. As Dr Richards Bandler frequently points out "Brains aren't designed to get results; they just go in directions".

So how can we use this knowledge to help improve our self-esteem an overall mental state? In reality, its simply a case of learning your ABC's I.e. learning the sequence of the Antecedent, Behavior and Consequence. I have explained these concepts in greater detail within previous books, so I'll just stick to the technique here so you can implement it when it comes to negative self-talk.

Thought Pattern Interrupts

The idea is to disrupt a negative thought pattern as early on in the cycle or sequence as possible, more specifically between the trigger and operation phase. Regardless, it must be completed before the testing phase of the condition, to say that you must disrupt it before the mind tries to test the original assumption, otherwise any attempt to break the sequence will be of little use as the pattern is almost completed.

The pattern interrupts aren't difficult to implement and its simply about stopping your train of thought and thinking about something different. It's a case of "butting in" on your own thought process and the conversation occurring within your own head. You are simply trying to change the direction of the mind and reprogram it as you do. You are not removing the old pattern per se, but rather redirecting around it.

To use an example from an earlier chapter regarding accomplishments. If you wish to stop viewing others as continually better than yourself.

You need to stop focusing on THEIR results, but rather focus on YOURS instead. You need to implement a thought pattern interrupt when you feel yourself becoming conscious of the gap in your perceived abilities. The following steps can help greatly with this:

1. Not Holding Back

The aim is to ensure the interrupt is as big and bold as possible. If there is one mistake I see from people who try this method, is that they are too weak with their disrupting action, and it isn't enough to fully divert their thinking. This is especially true regarding a long term, entrenched belief or pattern of thought which they are trying to break I.e. I'm not as good as everyone else. Try a loud clap of the hands or harsh cough whenever you feel this emotion as a significant interrupt.

2. Time it Correctly

You need to ensure you catch the "trigger phase" as accurately as you can, as it will be key to identifying when you need to employ the pattern disrupt. In essence, this should be directly after the original thought is spotted.

This stimulus/response window is typically a very short period of time. So you really have to be a keen observant throughout the day to catch them when they do occur. This can often be a thought or memory which pops into the mind which starts the negative cycle of thinking.

If you allow it to continue, your emotions and physiology will start to change. At this point it will be too late. You have to become proficient at catching it right before this transition takes place I.e immediately following the trigger thought/memory, and replace your momentary behavior to a more positive one.

3. Rinse & Repeat

Simply catching the cycle once will not be enough for most entrenched poorly held beliefs. The real payoff comes from repeating this cycle over and over until the new thinking pattern becomes habitual, and you start to see the results you are looking for I.e. a more realistic and positive outlook towards yourself.

So ensure you perform whatever interrupt you have chosen until it becomes second nature to you, until you no longer have to think about it. You have to bring the skill into the "Unconscious Competence" phase when performing it. That is when the new direction of thought and subsequent behavior will properly take hold.

This general approach was taken from hypnotherapists such as Milton Erickson who used pattern interrupts to disrupt the waking thinking patterns of their participants. They would lead a persons inner monologue down a familiar path before disrupting the line of questioning, leaving the persons unconscious mind waiting for the logical next step of the pattern, but it never comes. This can be a powerful enough confusion of the mind which puts a certain percentage of the population into a hypnotic trance.

You are not attempting to go this far with yourself, and it's almost impossible to do it on your own. However the general thought pattern interrupt is designed to work along the same lines. But this time to disrupt a familiar negative thought pattern and replace it with a positive more beneficial one.

Understanding that you will almost certainty be running negative and automatic negative thinking patterns is half of the battle. Breaking them is quite another fight altogether. It requires tools such as thought pattern interrupts to ensure newer and more positive upgrades are embedded into your psyche. So make sure you are cognizant of putting this effective cognitive trick into practice throughout the day as much as you can.

CHAPTER 6: THE BENEFITS OF CATASTROPHIZING

"A women is like a tea bag, you never know how strong she is until she gets in hot water"

(Eleanor Roosevelt)

In the previous chapter we discussed the importance of not letting negative thinking patterns remain in your mind indefinitely. Most of these patterns are now so ingrained into the synapses of the brain, they pretty much run on autopilot each day. This is why its so important to consciously break them. However, there is one instance where this catastrophizing behaviour can actually be beneficial.

I'll admit this is more of a confidence boosting exercise, rather than a complete self-esteem overhaul. In truth, its simply a strategy which can put your mind at ease for a multitude of situations. In this sense, I find it extremely useful for building ones own self-esteem as a by product. This is a trick to ultimately worry less. If you achieve this, you will just find yourself acting in a more harmonious and beneficial manner by proxy.

As we have already seen, most people use this concept of catastrophizing in the wrong way. They easily enter negative thinking spirals by default, which is why they are so difficult to avoid. If you are not careful, just the slightest misconception or negative connotation towards an event, can have you extrapolating out near disastrous outcomes in no time. My aim for this chapter is to show you how to use this natural tendency to your benefit.

This requires taking these negative trains of thought to their natural conclusion. You are already thinking of every bad outcome to begin with, so going one step further is not too much to ask. Let me give you an example. When I was initially starting up my consulting business, I had to employ a handful of staff to take care of all admin and house keeping tasks. This freed me up to deal with existing clients, as well as perform business development activities in order to attract new ones.

I would constantly worry about how I was going to make payroll each month, even though I knew we had several months of capital allocated to cover such costs. My main worry though, was actually the thought of one of my staff quitting, and leaving me with nobody to invoice my clients. Worst still, what if they took all of this sensitive information to a rival company and left me with nothing?

One day I decided that enough was enough and sat down to really think this situation through. I intimately explored every detail of this worst case scenario and lived out each outcome in my mind. I realized that in such a circumstance, I would simply have to find someone new, and start from scratch finding new clients all over again. This would give me the opportunity to find a new rock star employee as well as sharpen my sales skills. This actually started to seem quite an attractive situation.

But in reality, I came to the conclusion that all I really needed to do was get my staff to sign NDA's and client poaching clauses, as well as systematize their work & I'd be protected. Sure enough, within 6 months of doing this, my secretary quit to work for another company agreeing to keep all client information confidential. I then hired another lady to do the job and she learnt the systems and procedures within a week.

Nothing is ever as bad as it seems to be, or we project that its going to be. In fact, once you go through this worst case planning exercise, anything less than a disaster seems like a win. This greatly increases a persons confidence in their day-to-day lives, allowing them to move forward without all of the mental anguish which once held them back.

Remember its always beneficial to keep the old Zen Master in mind. To remind yourself of the old Taoist story of the farmer and his son. If you do not know it, the fable goes something like this:

There once was an old farmer who worked his crops with the aid of a trusty horse. One day the horse ran away, and the villagers lamented "What bad luck that is!".

The Zen master simply replied "We'll see".

The following day the horse returns, bringing with it three additional wild horses. To which the villagers cheered "How wonderful!".

The Zen master once again replied "We'll see".

A week later the farmer gives one of the horses to his son as a gift on his sixteenth birthday. The villagers reply, "Oh, how lovely, the boy got a horse!"

The Zen master says, "We'll see."

A few days later the boy gets thrown off the horse and breaks his leg. All of the villagers again lament, "How terrible!"

The Zen master replies, "We'll see."

The village is then visited by military officers who draft all the young men to go fight in the war. But the boy can't go as his leg is in a cast. The villagers say, "How lucky that is!"

The Zen master says, (you guessed it) "We'll see...."

This story automatically springs to mind whenever I view a situation as either being very good or bad. It's another pattern interrupt I've imprinted into my own thinking over the years. The words "We'll see" naturally pop into my mind whenever I feel a negative thinking spiral begins to occur.

Its of course good to keep an even keel when it comes to viewing extreme situations as inherently negative or positive. But most critical when catastrophizing events in your mind. Sit down and analyze these instances and plan for the worst. If you experience them in your head first, you will become much less afraid of them playing out in your physical reality.

You may even become disappointed if they don't! Hardships and troubles are the only true way to grow our characters and expand our comfort zones. Dealing with these instances in our minds and perhaps in "real life" is therefore the stepping stones to a stronger resolve, and ultimately a better life.

CHAPTER 7: POSITIVE ANCHORING & FRAMING TECHNIQUES

"Instead of becoming a victim in your life, become a student in your life, and watch yourself become a better women for it"

(Brittney Moses)

The following are popular psychological techniques to help you cultivate a more positive mindset and outlook on life. I include them here as I have found them to be some of the most effective in not only my own life, but countless others too. The strategies I'm referring to are "anchoring" and "framing". They can be extremely effective in building confidence and self-esteem so lets explore them in more detail.

Basic Anchoring

Anchoring is designed to help a person induce a beneficial emotional state. Its used to get a person into that confident or calm state of mind conducive for optimal experience and behavior. It involves "tricking" the mind into thinking that you are experiencing a flow state on demand. There are other slightly more complex and long winded ways to do this, but for now, let's look at the simple anchoring method.

Try to think of a time when you were extremely excited, confident or calm. This might be when you are enjoying dinner with family/friends, a good movie or achieving success in any given task. Anything which elicits this positive emotional reaction, the type that gives you butterflies in your stomach. Picture the moment in your head and be as vivid as possible, noticing all the sights, sounds and senses you experience at the time. Build a sensory neurological road map of the event.

Now the trick is to "anchor" this emotional snapshot which can be done using some form of touch or word, but in this case, try using your own hands and fingers as I find it to be the easiest way to do it. It certainly worked for me.

Its best to take the index and middle fingers of your left hand, and grasp them in the palm of your right hand. Now gently squeeze your fingers two times with a second or so pause in between. However, on the second squeeze try to bring in the picture and emotions from the experience you recalled above, the happy, confident place you prepared in your mind. Again the clearer the better.

Now try the finger squeezes once more, although this time the happy, confident emotional feeling of the positive picture on the second squeeze doubles. Then do it again, and it triples! Keep doing this until you feel an automatic rush of these positive emotions on every second squeeze of the fingers.

Essentially, what you have now done is anchor that positive feeling to a finger squeeze which can be recalled at any time. This works best for me when I am having a bad day and I want to elicit the feelings of a much more productive time. Or when heading into a meeting and I need to feel more confident and assured. I have trained two different types of finger squeeze, and have anchored a different feeling on each. One which makes me extremely confident, the other extremely calm.

All you are doing here is a form of neurological "copy and paste" of these thoughts and emotions. The primal limbic regions of the brain has no concept of time, it just recalls emotional input and helps the body experience them in the here and now. The mind and body will happily experience them again, as if they are happening now if you train it to, which this simple finger squeeze can do.

This basic method of anchoring positive emotions and feelings to recall on demand is one thing, it helps give you that momentary hit of calmness or confidence in any situation. However, there is another technique that I have used to good effect, but this time to downplay and remove negative emotions. It's the other side of the emotional coin and just as important, if not more so when developing higher levels of confidence and self-esteem.

Framing Techniques

Framing techniques usually fit in well with many other psychological strategies. Framing complements just about everything in the way it can amplify or deamplify emotional states by rebuilding pathways within the limbic region of the brain, more specifically between the amygdala and hippocampus.

Before I dive into the specifics of applying the framing techniques, it's wise to identify what we are dealing with in terms of "frames of reference" from an emotional stand point. As we have seen in earlier chapters, humans tend to learn lessons and ascribe meaning to things due to the events surrounding that situation. More specifically the memories we have regarding them, especially those from childhood.

If you think about it, both your life's past memories and future projections are nothing more than a show real, a filmstrip much like the negatives you see on those old movie projectors. They are just snapshots of events that we attribute meaning too after the fact. However, what people fail to realize is that meaning or emotional connection you may have related to something, may not be accurate and can be changed.

You've heard of the saying "If it's true for you, then it's true". That is a suggestion of projection of reality into the world, and is more of an observation within quantum mechanics. But it couldn't be more true in an experiential sense, especially when it comes to feelings and emotions. What is happening in your brain is the hippocampus is storing this long term memory data, whilst the amygdala is producing the emotions associated with it.

Although very close together anatomically, these two regions still need to communicate to produce the complete picture of the event with the emotions/meanings also attached. Sometimes they get this wrong, and you can certainly alter this association if you do not like what you see, or more accurately, what you feel.

Framing Negative Emotions

I believe the best place to start with framing is to remove or deamplify negative connotations to events which are holding you back. Start by thinking of a time that you perceived something to have gone badly, something that didn't turn out well and you now have a negative outlook towards. This might be failing your driving test or an interview that didn't go well.

This will unearth this negative memory from your hippocampus, and its now being displayed as a picture or short video reel within your prefrontal cortex, the rational part of the brain which makes sense of it. Additionally, the amygdala will be asked for the emotional data and will provide it as such. This will be negative emotions of fear, anxiety or disappointment most likely. Again, the amygdala has no real sense of time, so the emotions will feel fresh as if the event was happening again in the here and now.

Let's use the example of a failed driving test. You may have prepared thoroughly and done all of the turns perfectly with your instructor in the weeks leading up to the test. However, on the day of exam you arrived at the driving school late due to bad weather and heavy traffic, you were flustered and in a rush as a result. Certainly not a calm state ready to get on the road yourself.

Now form a picture of the event in your mind, make it one clear snapshot or frame that really sums up and encapsulates the moment. It might be you stalling the car on a hill start or sitting in the parking lot afterwards when feeling dejected. Whatever it is, form a picture of it.

Now take a step back from the situation. If you were looking at the picture through your own eyes, then start to view it from a third person perspective, looking down on the image from the corner of the frame. If you were already withdrawn from the image, than take an even further step back, and view it from an even greater detached position from say a little way down the street.

You should now be able to see yourself clearly in this picture, a frame that perfectly represents you failing your driving test that day. However, what you want to do now is actually blur the image a little, make it grainy and black and white like an old film negative I described previously. Put a physical frame around it, something like an old fashioned stainless steel frame you see in grand mansions in movies. The picture should now be seen to have a different texture, a pastel paint look perhaps.

The next thing to do is put this picture up on the wall. This may be in an art gallery for instance, anywhere people will glance at it before they move along with what they are doing without any real interest.

Finally, start to think about that memory/image once more in your mind. What you should find is that it has noticeably decreased in negative emotion. It may still feel a little uncomfortable, but nothing like what it used to! The trick is to go back and do this again with the same scenario, with that same image and any other images that may be linked to the memory. Put them all up on the wall beside one another, and see how they no longer elicit the same emotions they once did. They are now simply old pictures on a wall.

Framing Positive Emotions

The previous advice on framing negative past situations should have helped you view past traumatic events in a much more neutral and objective light, robbing them of their emotional baggage, and letting you move on with your life. Although there are times when you want to do the reverse I.e. framing moments in a more positive manner. This simply means you will again be taking previous events and situations from your past, but this time amplifying their meaning and effect.

For me it was about anchoring and triggering more positive emotions onto milestones that I had made in my business life, in order to fuel further progress, and to feed into my positive feedback loops. That is what is great about your life, you can use these techniques to completely design and direct it in any direction you wish.

So back to the positive framing strategy. When you are attempting to prepare yourself for an important upcoming event such as an interview, business meeting and the like, you first need to imagine yourself in a plain and empty room. Ask yourself "In what way would I like the people at this event to view me?" The image you have in your mind will be the image you are starting to construct here. Don't force it, just start to build the situation, your movements and body language, and how you see yourself acting in general.

Now watch the picture unfold as the situation is going extremely well, you are confidently conducting the meeting. People are really enjoying and appreciating the way you are delivering your speech, and may even be giving you light applause and congratulations. Watch how you confidently accept the adulation with a smile and straight back.

Now put this powerful, confident and calm image into the situation and surroundings of the upcoming event. Put yourself right there, see the visuals, the colors and textures of the room. Smell your favorite perfume on yourself to further increase assurance. Be as vivid as possible with this, once again see yourself completely convincing everybody in the room with what you are saying. See them smiling and laughing at your jokes.

Now blow this image up to 100 feet in diameter and watch it on an LCD screen directly in front of you within the empty room. It's so large that it fills an entire wall! The next step is to take a big stride into the picture, merge yourself with the digital image on the screen. Experience the situation through your own eyes, you are now thinking and feeling every sight, sound and emotion as if it were happening to you right now. Take as long as you like, soaking in the feelings of the super confident and calm person . This is your true self-image.

Rehearse this as many times as you like and for as many situations as you wish. You should start to automatically put yourself in the confidant persons shoes as it will feel so natural to you, as you have now been there many times before. Again, the mind doesn't know the difference between an imagined or "real" event. You are simply littering your future film reel with positive success stories from an emotional standpoint. When you actually get there, it will seem very familiar, and natural to behave in that way.

CHAPTER 8: AFFIRMATIONS & ASSERTIVENESS TRAINING

"Disciplining yourself to do what you know is right and important, although difficult, is the highroad to pride, self-esteem and personal satisfaction"

(Margret Thatcher)

During my college years I spent much time studying the intricacies of the various personality types. Much of this work stems from Carl Jung's original 4 archetypes, or models of human behavior. These being the King, Warrior, Magician and Lover. This can further be broken down more specifically on an individual level by the Myers-Briggs 4-letter typing method, which are as follows:

1. Extraversion vs Introversion

2. Sensing vs Intuition

3. Thinking vs Feeling

4. Judgment vs Perception

Myers & Briggs (a mother and daughter psychologist team) presented the theory that every person will lean more heavily towards one of these two preferences. Everyone will display tendencies of each from time to time, but one will dominate for the most part. So by answering a set of inventory questions, you can attain a personal score, which will give you your individual 4-letter personality type.

For instance, having the preference of ISFP, will mean you predominantly exhibit the traits of an Introverted, Sensing, Feeling and Perception orientated person. This is of course somewhat of a simplification of the complex nature of personality, but a good place to start none-the-less. Large corporations will give new employees more detailed versions of this test in order to see where they may best fit into the company.

Its no secret that women tend to fall more on the feminine side of these traits. We typically exhibit more introverted, intuitive and feeling characteristics. We are also much more agreeable on average, compared with men for instance. Yes there are outliers at the extremes, but this is typically the case.

This is both a benefit and downside depending on what situation you are in. Its a plus if you work in the humanities, or being a nurse or primary school teacher for instance, as these positions require higher degrees of empathy to perform well. Feminine tendencies can be much less beneficial in the historically male dominated sectors though. In fact, it has been shown to be highly negatively correlated towards success in the business world. I certainly learned this the hard way when I entered the cut and thrust of the consulting game. This doesn't mean we can't excel in these fields, we simply have to know how to prepare properly.

One of my favourite things to do now, is to coach other women on how to improve their assertiveness in this sense. How to negotiate things firmly and properly to get what they want from life (when its needed), instead of always leaning towards keeping the peace. This is critical for those entering the fields of finance or law for instance, and the two best ways I find to do this is with affirmations and basic assertiveness training.

Affirmations

Lets start with affirmations. When done correctly, they are very effective. They are another form of neurological mapping which helps ingrain positive pathways into the synapses of the brain. When done often enough they become your default mindset, they replace any existing negative thought patterns with much more beneficial ones. This will take some work and will feel strange at first, but stick with them and they will soon become second nature.

You will be participating in an enormous amount of self-talk throughout the day anyway, so you may as well frame this chatter in a positive light to begin with. If you do so, you will find yourself operating in a much more effective manner, able to deflect any negative behavior or criticism which comes your way. You will have a set of guiding values and principles to fall back on, instead of getting swept up by the wind in which ever direction it may be blowing.

Here are some examples of high level affirmations a person might perform:

- I deserve to be happy and successful

- I am free to make my own choices in life

- I have the power to change my circumstances

Some more specific examples relating to overall levels of confidence and self-esteem may include:

- I act with confidence throughout the day, as I strive for my goals

- I am confident in any situation I find myself in

- I love meeting and interacting with new people

You can create any combination of statements which work for you best. My advice would be to come up with the ten which resonate with your current mindset and situation the most. Write down 5-7 general confidence boosting affirmations which may remain throughout your life. But 3-4 which pertain to something specific you are dealing with right now. This may be a rough relationship break up for instance, or a tough workplace environment.

Just be sure to write them in the present tense and in a positive manner, as if you have already achieved the intent of the statement. Some more examples may include:

- I am successful right now

- I am strong enough to be on my own

- This job is challenging, but I am able to handle it easily

Again, ensure you write these down on a note pad with a pen or pencil. Studies show that we internalize things we write down more deeply, as the act of moving the pen etches them into the synapses of the brain. It can be up to 70% more efficient then typing them out for instance, which is much less personable. Once you have your list, keep them by your bedside and read them aloud each morning and night. Your subconscious mind is most open during these time periods, so your positive affirmations will have the best chance to sink in.

Assertiveness Tips

As I mentioned, one of my main joys in life is getting other women across the goal line in terms of business/career success. In fact, any form of life experience they are struggling with. Almost anything can be made better with a little more sternness on the part of the individual, to stand up for what they want. I'm not saying be pushy, assertiveness is rather having the confidence to be your true self.

Even though we typically fall on the more sensitive side of the personality paradigms, this is not an excuse for getting poor results in the world. Being heavily introverted for instance, doesn't mean you should be taken advantage of, or continually put the needs of others before your own. Being self-ish in terms of personal success is your duty. Its actually a very selfless act. You can't help anybody if you do not have the means to contribute.

Long gone are the days when the man was the sole breadwinner in the family. Many women are choosing to stay single or unmarried for longer than ever now, in order to more easily focus on a career path. In this sense, assertive personality traits are vital. Corporate positions and the business world are getting more competitive by the day, so you need to know how to compete properly.

Its difficult to distill this form of training into tidbits within a book. But areas you should be studying include, communication patterns (assertive, passive, aggressive etc), leadership behaviors, body language reading, persuasion and negotiation tactics, being able to say "no" in difficult situations without the feeling of guilt. Being able to hold a room with the correct vocabulary and voice tonality.

There are plenty of resources online and seminars within your area which can help you develop these characteristics. Its simply about identification of what aspects of your personality you need to improve upon. Like always, there's no shame in doing this, its a self-help activity which will improve literally every area of your life. Having a stronger constitution in face of troubles, or just everyday life for that matter, allows you to reap that much more from the interactions you'll have.

It's not about screwing anyone over, its simply getting whats right for you. Nobody will be angered by this, they will likely be thankful you can be more straight and frank with them. Your friends and family will be especially grateful, as your progress positively affects those around you the most. I therefore give you the permission to act more assertively and get what you want. Try it out, your self-esteem will start to sky rocket when you do!

CONCLUSION

"This is a chapter of my story where I trade a lifetime of fear, for a lifetime of freedom, by learning how to fight. Its the part where I transform from victim to hero on every page that I write for the rest of my life"

(Christy Ann Martine)

Simply put, self-esteem underpins all behaviour, good and bad. Raising it, and maintaining high levels is critical to leading a harmonious life, let alone achieving any tangible success. In reality, it doesn't matter if you are male or female, the playbook is largely the same. Yes there are some subtle differences in an experiential sense between the sexes, but we are all humans at the end of the day. We learn, grow and develop in exactly the same way, through experience.

Its clear by now that I view the inner workings of the mind to be a critical component to all of this, its how we interpret these experiences which matters. However, you don't have to be a psychologist to know that what you perceive inside of yourself, is what you'll project outwards, and ultimately, what you'll receive back in return. Manifesting anything isn't a one way street, but rather a boomerangs journey so to speak.

This is why cultivating a positive mindset is critical, which is largely determined by ascribing the correct, or should I say most beneficial, meanings to the events which happen to us. We can't control everything which occurs in our environment, but we can control our outlook on them, and certainly how we'll react to them. We can even go back and fix these broken instances in our minds with framing techniques.

It will certainly require some effort on your part, but what could be more rewarding work than legitimately achieving higher levels of self-esteem? "Self-Confidence is not taught or learned; it is earned by surpassing your own self-limitations" as John Raynolds correctly states. Yes you will naturally overcome some of your negative conditioning with time, but the passive approach is never the best one. Why not take the bull by the horns and direct your life in the manner you wish, and right now.

Its impossible to calculate the extent of the payoffs you may reap by doing so. Increasing your overall self-esteem impacts every minor detail of your day. It effects every interaction large and small. The benefits compound and become exponential before long. Its easier to see this with specific physical attributes, say when a teenager firsts gets their braces removed. They go from a shy, introverted kid, to chatty and smiley extrovert over night. I know this one all too well!

However, its the nagging psychological tendencies which dwell in our minds for years which can do the most damage, as they can be very hard to spot. They are often egoic elements of your psyche, pretending to keep you safe, but in reality, they are holding you back. This is where the tips and techniques within this book can really help. In identifying these thinking patterns and replacing them with much more positive ones.

Life then just becomes a downhill bicycle ride. When you think more of yourself, automatically acting in ways which benefits you most, just seems natural. Its becomes the path of least resistance. Self-Sabotaging behaviour disappears and you get propelled forward like never before. So ensure you begin putting these strategies into practice right away, you will thank yourself in the long run I promise you.

BONUS CHAPTERS

(From 'Emotional Intelligence: A Psychologist's Guide')

CHAPTER 4: TAKING INVENTORY OF YOUR EMOTIONAL STATE

"Educating the mind without educating the heart is
no education at all"

(Aristotle)

One of the most important things you can do when initially starting out on your emotional intelligence enhancing journey is to take stock of what you are currently feeling. There is no right or wrong answers here in terms of what come up. As our limbic legacy show us, humans are inherently emotional creatures and suppressing them is almost impossible to do entirely.

However you do have control over the way you react to these tendencies, the thoughts and behaviors after the fact. The following factors should help you take a closer look into how to identify and deal with these feelings when they do arise to ultimately move you to the next level in your E.Q. journey.

Acknowledge Your Emotions

The first thing to do when attempting to increase your personal E.Q. levels is to get good at acknowledging and perceiving the emotions that you are feeling. This is the starting point for every model and framework of E.Q.

Whenever I feel an emotion arise within me I always take a pause and acknowledge its presence, I take a moment and really feel it so I can understand and label it in my mind. This isn't the same as reacting or acting upon the emotion just yet, but I want to know why it may have arisen and if it could be useful to me. If it's a feeling of anger, fear or frustration I do not deny or try to hide it, but instead acknowledge its presence and dismiss it as not being productive and move on.

If you start to dwell on emotions such as these you will quickly fall into a negative spiral thought process that will have you framing everything in a pessimistic light before you know it. I used to play out entire imaginary scenarios in my head of something going badly and the knock-on effects that I 'knew' it would have, only to realize that it NEVER worked out that badly and that I'd fabricated it all in my mind. Sound familiar?

If on the other hand it is an emotion of excitement, joy or anticipation, I also pause for a moment, acknowledge and label what it is that I'm feeling and try to cultivate and utilize it if I think it will benefit the situation such as situational empathy (which we will get onto later).

It is also important to take responsibility for these emotions that you are feeling either way, good or bad. Know that it is something inside of you which is eliciting such a response and that you have to deal with it and not sweep it under the carpet so to speak. This is usually the most challenging step for people, but it is also the most rewarding. Yes it maybe some outside influence or stimulus that sparked the response in the first place, but remember that the emotions you are feeling are coming from within you and that it's your responsibility to deal with them

Understand That You Are Not Your Emotions

So following on from that, you also need to constantly remind yourself that the emotions which arise within you and the conscious entity which interprets them are two very different things. Most people walk around in somewhat of a waking sleep for the most part completely at the mercy of any feeling, thought or emotion that pops into their head.

You have to understand that many thoughts and emotions will pass through you almost on a second by second basis, but again it's entirely your choice on how you perceive and choose to react to them.

There is also a very large egoic element to this process as well. Thoughts and feelings of jealously for another person or fear of performing a task is really just your ego trying to keep your preconceived notions about the world intact and keep you operating within your comfort zone. This is a topic for much greater discussion i.e. regarding the tactics to counteract such self-sabotaging behavior, but needless to say that detaching yourself from your overall emotional state is very a beneficial thing to do.

Learn to Forgive Yourself & Others

"Life becomes easier when you learn to accept an
apology you never got"

(Robert Brault)

Again, along the same lines as letting go of a negative emotion
that arises within you, people have a great tendency to hold
onto what they perceive to be negative acts that they have either
committed themselves or others against them. Holding onto
this ill feeling again serves absolutely no purpose to you in the
immediate future and certainly not the long run. *"Holding onto
anger is like drinking poison and expecting the other person to die"* as the
Buddha so aptly put it.

If there was one thing that got me ahead in my business life so
quickly it was this concept. Once I stopped getting caught up
with what I thought I deserved from a situation or others around
me and started pushing ahead regardless, I made so much more
progress. You can't stop and throw stones at every dog that barks,
and that includes yourself when you mess up.

This isn't just applicable to adult and business life either, it's relates
to everyone young or old. If I had taken heed of this advice
when I was growing up I know I would have had better overall
relationships with school/college friends and family alike. That's
not to say things were necessarily that bad, but they could have

been better, or at least I could have saved myself a great deal of heart ache and stress along the way.

Don't Get Involved in Negative Self-Talk

As I mentioned above, letting negative self talk get out of hand is a very bad habit to take up. I would say that it is the one thing that plagues humanity more than anything. We often talk ourselves out of things before we've had a chance to start them. Again this comes down to letting negative thoughts and emotions cloud our thinking to a point of almost no escape. You have to stop this in its tracks as quickly as possible if you want to build high overall levels of emotional intelligence.

This also includes negative self-talk and 'gossip' regarding other people. In danger of sounding like one of your parents or school teachers here, you don't need me to tell you this is a worthless exercise and one that will ultimately bring your E.Q. level down with it. No one is perfect; just make a point of catching yourself when you start to talk in this way.

Also along the same lines as the above, you must try and do your best not to judge others where ever possible. This actually freed me greatly in a psychological sense when I managed to stop doing it a few years ago. I never thought of myself as an overly judgmental person but I still realized I would do it from time to time. But stopping myself altogether from judging anyone I came across in even the smallest way saves me so much mental energy and almost certain daily miss judgment.

Nowadays I simply let others go about their day in their own way without even the slightest judging thought about their behavior. That is not to say that I tolerate bad behavior or that I do not try and empathize with people and attempt to understand their situation better, which is critical to building fruitful relationships. But I don't judge them with regards to how they got to where they are, I never walked in their shoes or went through the struggles they did so I let them do the talking on this one.

Again this isn't some "holier than thou" situation, I'm not perfect and do very occasionally catch myself automatically judging someone. I just now catch it very early and stop myself in my tracks straight away. It's so much more liberating when you do.

BONUS CHAPTER

(From 'Jealousy: A Psychologist's Guide')

CHAPTER 5: RAISING YOUR OVERALL SELF-ESTEEM

"A competent and self-confident person is incapable of jealousy in anything. Jealousy is invariably a symptom of neurotic insecurity"

(Robert Heinlein)

The following passage is an adaptation from a chapter I wrote within *"Manipulation: A Psychologists Guide"*. However it is very apt for a discussion on jealousy, hence why I have included and expanded upon it here. I plan to write an entire book solely dedicated to the notion of raising overall self-confidence, especially with regards to women, as its such an important trait to develop.

If there is one true antidote to manipulative behavior in general, which includes jealousy, it is in raising ones own self-esteem and self-worth. Its the one overriding factor which protects you from pretty much all negative emotions which arise within you, as well as those emanating from others.

It's not some clever tactic or trick to deflect negative comments or anything like that, but rather raising your own self-confidence aids in diffusing the impact jealous actions have on you from the get-go. It inoculates you from ever being affected by negative behavior in the first place, as these forms of feelings are typically unconscious acts played out by those experiencing low confidence or temporary vulnerability.

Nobody will truly feel jealous if they have a high regard for themselves. In truth, nothing is more important than how you think and feel about yourself, that goes for relationships as well as life in general.

Handle Your Inner Critic

You have an inner critic, everyone does. Listening to this voice can aid in getting things done or helps you do the things that will gain acceptance from other people. But this inner critic can also kill your self-esteem if you let it. If you permit this egoic element of your personality to get out of hand.

I have described the importance of separating the "thinker" from the "feeler" within you in previous books. Needless to say that over thinking situations is not a good thing to be doing, I would go as far to say its the biggest plight on human civilization today.

It is normal for your inner voice to suggest both positive and negative thoughts. It's not about blocking out the noise. But rather analyzing what you are thinking, and if it is of any benefit to you? If it isn't, then it's important to prevent yourself from going down the rabbit hole of negative and spiraling imaginary scenarios.

Refocus those negative thoughts into something constructive and happier.

Cultivate a Gratitude Mindset

I used to think that being grateful for the sake of it was silly. Why would I appreciate everything I had in my life now? My goals were much larger and loftier. Wouldn't this be me thinking small and making do? Absolutely not! The mind works in a way to serve you more of what you are currently experiencing now. If you are constantly in a state of fear and worry, guess what. Your subconscious will simply serve you up more to be fearful and worried about.

On the other hand, if you are extremely positive and grateful in the here and now, the mind goes to work in finding you more of the same! The subconscious doesn't know the difference between feeling great because you just won the lottery, are being ecstatic simply to be alive. It works in feelings, emotions and imagery.

In this regard, learning to appreciate yourself, and all of the good things about your life, including your current relationship, is a great exercise to do. As a bonus to this, when you feel good about yourself and grateful for the things that you do have large or small, your mind won't have room to entertain negative thoughts.

Most of the suffering people go through in their lives is imaginary anyway. It's created from the dissonance between where they are and where they think they would like to be. But that is a false horizon, if you can't be happy with the journey then you will never be content with wherever you are heading, as there will always be the next thing when you get there.

Again, the trick is to be happy now. I know this sounds over simplified and easier said then done, but it really is the one thing which gave me the most joy in life when I was struggling with my business in the early days.

It has been shown that the top business professionals in the world do this (and all successful people in general). If they are currently at point 'B' in their lives, they do not look forward to point 'C' and say "look how far I have to go." As I mentioned previously, this is just a conceptual place like the horizon of the earth. Every time you try to chase after it, it disappears further into the distance.

Instead, what these people do is look back at point 'A' to where they started and say "hey, look how far I have come!" This is a subtle change of outlook but I promise you, if you do make this one adjustment in your thinking your whole outlook on life will change, and for the better. You will instantly start feeling grateful and satisfied with your current lot and much less frustrated with not yet being where you think you should be. Remember that the subconscious aims to serve you more of what you are felling right now. If you are abundantly happy and grateful for what is in your present existence, then it will go to work on finding other such situations to bring your way.

My previous business partner used to valet his car outside of his favorite restaurant in the city each week. However he could never understand why the parking attendant would always place his car two blocks away, instead of just across the road as he'd instructed. He would get so frustrated by having to wait an extra 5 minutes for his vehicle each time, it almost sent him into a frenzy. He would ask me what he should do about it, as he noticed I was much calmer in similar situations.

I simply asked him to think about it for a moment. What would he rather, be a well paid businessman who had the opportunity to valet his top of the range BMW at his favorite restaurant each week. But have to wait an extra five minutes for it each time he left. Or be the guy who has to valet cars and survive off tips for a living? His outlook on the situation immediately changed. "You're right he replied, what was I thinking? I'll give the guy a break from now on".

Put Things Into Writing

You can also write down the things that you like about yourself in a journal, the positive traits you have and situations they affect. When you are feeling low, or when the day is not turning out as well as you'd hoped, or when negative thoughts begin to creep into your mind, take out your list and re-read them. You can update this list daily, or whenever you discover something new and positive about yourself.

It's a good idea to start your day with going over these statements as they work a little like affirmations. You are cultivating the positive emotions surrounding these attributes or events and allowing you to feel them again in the here and now. Remember the brain has no way of telling the difference with regards to emotions I.e. the event could be happening now, 10 years ago or some way into the future!

Stop Being a Perfectionist

Aiming for perfection all of the time can be very destructive. Just like negative thoughts, perfectionism can paralyze you from getting things done due to your fear of not living up to a high standard you have set for yourself. This may also result in procrastination, thus, ending up not getting you the results you expected. This will bring your self-esteem crashing down if you let it.

Try making these alterations to your thinking to overcome perfectionism:

- *Strive for good enough.* Stop aiming for perfection, remember nobody's perfect. When you aim for perfection all of the time, you won't finish any task because you'll either wait for the right time or continue to work on the task until it turns out flawless (which will never happen).

- *Striving for perfection will only hurt you in the long run.* Remind yourself that life is not a fairy tale that always ends with *a happily ever after.* Learn to manage your expectations, because after all, this is real life. You have managed to deal with everything life has thrown at you up until this point, how do I know this? Because you are still alive reading this today. The true curve balls in life you will never see coming so there is absolutely no point in worrying about them today. You will deal with them at the time as you always have done, so stop worrying.

Look at Mistakes and Failure as Lessons

I will go into greater detail on this topic within the chapter on re-contextualization shortly. But for now, lets just say that it is inevitable that you will make mistakes from time to time. You will fail on some days. But the good thing about experiencing failures and committing mistakes is that there are lessons to be gleaned from them all.

There will always be positives you can take from every situation, you just have to find out what they are. Learn from them and internalize these things and come back stronger. "You either win or you learn" as they say. I couldn't agree more.

Similar to this, you always need to be trying something new. Get out of your comfort zone as much and as often as possible. This is the only true route to feeling content and successful in life. In having new experiences and learning new things that will feed into your positive confidence and self-esteem feedback loops.

They do not need to be big and scary all of the time, just small wins, incremental progress will do the job. As long as you are moving in the right direction, that is all that counts.

Stop Comparing Yourself to Others

You will never be good enough if you keep on comparing yourself with other people. You will never win because there's always someone better or there is always something more valuable to attain out there. You are only ever in a competition with yourself, to improve on the version of you from yesterday or a year ago.

Remember to always look back at 'A', not forward to 'C'. Look at how far you have come as a person with regards to your development. Other people are on their own journey, let them get on with it. Only you walk in your shoes, be proud of that and keep treading your own path.

Be Around People who are Supportive of You

This is fairly obvious but most people still do not take as much notice of this concept as they should. It's simple, don't hang around negative people who only see the things that you have done wrong. This includes jealous people!

It's said that you are the aggregate of the five people you most commonly associate with. Or show me your friends and I'll show you your future type of deal. This is because we adjust our behavior in line with these people accordingly. That goes for everything from mannerisms, speaking styles to the amount of money everyone is making. You will adjust your thermostat in all categories to usually meet the mean of this peer group.

So try to be around positive and high performance people, those who are willing to support you and lift you up. This is easier said then done with regards to close friends and family, but you do have to draw the line somewhere. Be with people who will pick you up when you fall and help you get back on your feet again.

Make a conscious effort to only socialize with those who encourage your progress and feed your confidence. It goes without saying that the jealous types will have a hard time with this. So be ruthless, remove them from your social groups or at least cut down your exposure to them whenever possible. Rising above needless gossip goes a long way in preventing the green eyed monster from ever rearing its ugly head!

Made in United States
Orlando, FL
28 November 2023

39681980R00057